Soccer Tactical Periodization
"Made Simple"
A Soccer Coaching Model
Adding Structure, Organization, Focus & Science To Coaching
Game Model = Training Model

By Marcus DiBernardo

Introduction

I wrote this book with the purpose of making the practice concept of "Tactical Periodization" simple and adaptable for coaches of all levels. Tactical periodization is a fantastic soccer-coaching concept, but it does not have to be exclusively for use in the professional soccer setting. I see great value in adapting the ideas of tactical periodization to fit all different types of coaching situations. Grasping the basics of tactical periodization will allow you to customize a practice program that works for you and your team. There is a reason why some of the world's top coaches believe in the process of "Tactical Periodization" - because it works. I guarantee "Tactical Periodization" will make you a better coach.

About The Author

Coach DiBernardo has been coaching the game of soccer for over 20 years. He has experience in both the men's and women's game at many levels. Coach DiBernardo's desire to coach came early on. His first coaching experience began at the young age of eighteen at his local soccer club in Durham, Connecticut. In the years to come, Coach DiBernardo would go on to lead numerous teams to many titles across the country. In 2011, he was named "National College Coach of The Year". Currently, Coach DiBernardo is the Founder and Director of an International Soccer Academy as well as a Head Men's College Soccer Coach.

Coach DiBernardo holds a number soccer diplomas and licenses. He is a member of the NSCAA Associate National Staff and considers himself a lifetime learner and active student of the game. He strongly believes, the better he can become as a coach, the more rounded the program experience he can design and share with his players.

Be sure to check out all of Coach DiBernardo's soccer books on Amazon.com. To date he has published over 25 titles on a number of soccer topics.

Table of Contents

1. What is Tactical Periodization?
2. Moments of The Game
3. Moments of The Game Sub-Principles
4. Offensive & Defensive Principles
5. Training Principles
6. Standard Morphocycle
7. Adapting Tactical Periodization To Fit Your Coaching Situation
8. One Week Sample Training Plans For Standard Morphocycle

What Is Tactical Periodization

Tactical periodization is a way of practicing that teaches the game to a specific game model. The game model is simply the way the coach wants the team to play. When watching teams like Barcelona, Arsenal, Dortmund and Real Madrid it is easy to identify their game model by the way they play. Tactical periodization provides a logical structure and specific organization for daily, weekly and season long training, which directly focuses on teaching to the game model. Tactical periodization teaches specifically to the game model and not only the game, all areas relate to the game model, which is the foundation of all training. In simple terms, this means every practice session will relate directly to how the team plays 11v11. Every player will train in their specific position during all exercises, focusing on the game model. Tactical periodization training breaks down the game model into the four moments of the game (offensive organization, attacking transition, defensive organization, defensive transition) along with defensive and attacking schemes. The game model is the idea of how the coach wants the team to play but in reality some adaptions may have to take place, since the game of soccer is complex and ever changing. It is better to choose a game model early in the season. This will allow the team to start working on a specific style of play and players will be able to train in their specific positions right away. The practice concept of tactical periodization should be looked at as a never-ending process that is carried out in weekly cycles called "morphocycles". A standard morphocycle is considered the space between games, normally a seven-day cycle. However, the cycle will vary depending on the match schedule. There will be times when a team might play multiple games in a week or have an extended break, at that point the morphocycle will change. The standard 7-day morphocycle will break-up the weeks training into daily tactical and physical training objectives, with the intent of obtaining optimum performance for the weekends match day.

Tactical periodization recognizes that the game of soccer is complex and contains many unpredictable and uncontrollable elements. The concept of peaking is not used in the theory of periodization. Instead the goal of tactical periodization is to stabilize "high-level successful play" from week to week. This is called the "Stabilization of Performance". Winning and losing in a one game situation can be the product of luck but over the duration of many games, the concept of "stabilization of successful play" can be seen. In order to construct your own tactical periodization program and game model, there are a series of principles you will need to study and define. <u>When teaching the game model the "moments of the game & sub-principles of the game must be introduced, learned and used in each and every training session</u>. Players must be able to identify the moments of the game in the actual game model in order to execute the game plan.

Moments of The Game

1) **Offensive Organization:** This is when the team keeps possession of the ball and circulates the ball with the objective of unbalancing the defense and creating scoring chances.

2) **Attacking Transition:** This is the moment the ball is recovered and possession is won. At this time the team begins to open up and prepares to keep possession or prepares to penetrate immediately if the opportunity presents itself. The first moments that the ball is won are very important because the opposition is disorganized and unbalanced. Transition at speed is very important at this point. The counter attack and even the counter off the counter are a major part of many modern game models. Jose Mourinho would make the point that "the moment the ball is won or lost is the most important time in the game".

3) **Defensive Organization:** The lines of defense will be defined with the back line, midfield line and forwards all working together as one collective unit. The objective of defensive organization is to stop the opponent's offensive organization, therefore eliminating goal-scoring chances.

4) **Defensive Transition:** This is moment when the ball is lost and the opponents gain possession. The first priority will be to put pressure on the ball, which will allow numbers to fill in behind the ball, making the defense difficult to breakdown. Immediate pressure on the ball can also create a turnover that can result in a counter attack.

Moments of The Game Sub-Principles

(Sub-Principles are Underlined - these principles should be taught in training in direct relation to the game model – Customize the sub-principles to fit your game model)

1) Offensive Organization - Sub-Principles – 3 Phases

1st Build Phase: The objective is to break through the opponent's defensive lines. This phase usually starts in the back with the keeper or defensive line working the ball out from the back.

Principles of 1st Building Phase: <u>Proper Player Positional Balance & Back Line of 3:</u> Center backs start to open up, wing backs push forward, defensive midfielder drops into gap between center backs looking to receive ball. When these movements happen the team is opening-up the field preparing to circulate the ball and keep possession. <u>Keeper With Good Feet:</u> Having a keeper with good technical ability with his feet helps in building from the back. The keeper can help switch the ball from side-to-side in order to relieve pressure. <u>Pass To Draw Defenders In:</u> Passing short will draw in the defense opening up longer more direct passes to advanced players. <u>Play Direct:</u> If defense has pressed multiple players high, look for longer options that bypass the pressure. **Principles of 2nd Building Phase**: This phase focuses on creating chances to score by creating imbalances or overloads against the defense. The 2nd phase is generally started in the midfield in the middle third of the field. The objective is to simply create scoring opportunities. Stretch The Field: It is important to have maximum field width created by the wingbacks or wingers and good depth provided by the forward, wingers or attacking center midfielder. Positional Switches of Players: Players who interchange and create attacking overloads will unbalance and confuse the defense, while creating a numerical advantage on attack, just be sure to have balance in the team when inter-changing. Occupy Different Lines: Wingers and wingbacks should take up different lines when attacking. Generally, one will cut inside and the other will provide attacking width outside. Positional Organization: The team in possession must create options and passing angles for player with the ball. **3rd Building Phase**: This is known as the "Scoring or Finishing Phase": This phase is characterized by scoring with efficiency while filling (running into) scoring zones in front of goal. The 3rd phase is initiated and takes place in the attacking 1/3 in front of goal. Crossing IQ: The crossing player needs to make intelligent decisions on the ball and possess a wide range of skills, he must be able to play balls on the ground, in-the air, hit bending balls, have the vision to pick out the open attackers, be accurate crossing to the near & far post and take on defenders 1v1 if needed. Effective Positioning in Box: Attacking runners must time their runs into the three designated attacking zones (zones are near post & far post 5 yards out from goal and a middle zone about 8 yards from goal) and not be waiting in the space for the ball to arrive. Ideally three players will attack and one player will be outside box looking for a poor clearance or rebound.

2) Defensive Transition: Sub-Principles

<u>Mental Commitment:</u> As soon as the ball is turned over the players must have a very strong commitment both mentally and physically to win the ball back. First, second and third efforts are required of players. <u>Team Recovery:</u> The team must work hard for each other and recover quickly behind the ball. <u>Quality Individual Defending</u> – Quality of 1v1 marking – it determines the team's ability to defend. <u>Defensive Block:</u> Close central space and gaps - force play wide or back – force play into areas to trap, pressure and create a counter. <u>Prevent Penetrating Balls Through & Behind The Back 4:</u> Priority is to have lines of depth over the offsides trap.

3) Defensive Organization: Sub-Principles (3 Phases)

1st Defensive Phase – <u>Stopping The Possession Build-Up:</u> This normally occurs when the keeper has the ball, a goal kick is given, the back four is opening up and starting to circulate the ball or when there is a throw-in for the opponents in their own defensive 1/3. <u>Defense Push Up:</u> The defense would need to press up the field and stop the team in possession from building out of the back. The idea would be to create a turnover or force a long ball to be played. <u>Press Hard In Targeted Areas:</u> Another way to stop the build up of possession would be to press hard in pre-designed areas "trapping areas".

2nd Defensive Phase:

<u>Multiple Lines of Defense:</u> To prevent the creation of scoring chances use multiple lines of defense depth. <u>Limit Space Between The Lines:</u>

Keep the space in-between the defensive lines small so the team shape is compact.

Defensive Shifting: The strong side (side the ball is on) should be compact with defenders, when the ball is shifted to the weak side the entire team must shift quickly to maintain compactness.

3rd Defensive Phase:

This phase takes place in the defensive 1/3 of the field as the opponents are trying to score. Multiple Lines of Depth: It is important to put a priority on defensive depth in the lines of players. Do Not Play A Rigid High Line for Offsides: Playing a high offside line is not the objective. It is better to emphasize depth compared to allowing space behind the back four. Cover Dangerous Areas In Box: Make sure defenders mark all the dangerous spaces in the box and the central area on top of the box (near post, far post, centrally and top of the box). Second Balls: It is very important to win all 2nd balls when the ball is played into dangerous areas.

4) Attacking Transition: Sub-Principles:

This phase takes place right when possession is regained. This is when the team attempts to take advantage of the oppositions defensive disorganization and unbalance. Ideally the creation of an immediate scoring opportunity off a turnover is the desired result. Direct Deep Ball: If a player can play an immediate deep ball (without a large amount of risk of a turnover) that will result in an opportunity on goal, he should do so. Offensive Organization: If the deep ball is not present with certainty, the team should go into offensive organization and build. <u>Mental Attitude To Attack:</u> The attitude and motivation to strike quickly must be present when the ball is just won.

<u>Fill All Three Channels:</u> Once the transition to attack has started, all three channels of the field should have players breaking into them, this allows the ball to work central to lateral or lateral to central. <u>Read The Defensive Line:</u> Make sure to take advantage of teams who push a high line and exploit the space behind them. In modern soccer, games are often decided on a team's quality in transition.

The Game Cycle: Four Moments of The Game

Offensive Organization
Possession to attract opponents

Relieve pressure and get ball long to penetrate if possible or relieve pressure and possess the ball and be patient

Circulate the ball to create spaces in the opponents defense

Offensive Transition
Take advantage of opponents disorganization

Game Cycle

Defensive Transition
Immediate pressure on the ball and slowing the attack

Keep good compact shape and force opponents into pressing areas

Immediately press the ball looking to create a turnover or allowing defenders to recover behind the ball

Defensive Organization
Aggressive Zonal Defending
Low Block

The moments of the game need to be identified and taught in each practice session's in-relation to the game model. Both coaches and players must be able to discuss the game model and break it down in terms of the moments of the game and sub-principles. Being able to apply the moments of the game and the transition or flow between the different moments to the game model, shows an understanding of the information in its applied form. Tactical periodization training sessions specifically work on the moments of the game individually and collectively as they fit into the game model as a whole. The moments of the game sub-principles can be customized to fit your own unique game model. Barcelona's objectives will be different than Real Madrid's objectives. However, both teams must be able to identify and understand the four moments of the game, the sub-principles and how those moments and principles relate to their specific game model.

Offensive & Defensive Principles

The next area of tactical periodization connected to the four moments of the game are the **"Offensive and Defensive Principles"**. These principles are fundamental concepts that help create the foundation, organization and structure of play for the game model when used with the four moments of the game. It is important to refer to these principles when teaching the game model.

Offensive Principles:

1. **Penetration** – When possession is won the team with the ball should look for the most dangerous forward penetrating pass that would lead to a goal or shot if realistic. This principle can get complicated because decision making on the ball is a complex process and must fit within the game model. A possession team may look forward but most often they will need to be patient before going forward. Penetrating balls are the priority but only if they are calculated and realistic. If a possession team forces direct passing too much, their style of play or game model will be compromised.

2. **Support**: The players on the ball must have teammates off the ball working hard to offer passing options. Top possession teams support each other extremely well with coordinated timed movement.

3. **Width**: In order to maintain possession and open up the defense, the ball must be worked from side to side. Switching the ball from side to side requires a team to play with width in possession.
4. **Mobility**: The ability of players to take people on 1v1 and use acceleration and speed help break down the defense. The interchanging of positions and movement off the ball serves to unbalance the defense.

Defensive Principles

1. **Delay:** When possession is lost the player closest to the ball must slow down the opponents attack. By delaying the attacker and stopping them from going forward with the ball, it allows other defenders to recover behind the ball and take up a solid defensive team shape behind the ball.
2. **Support in Defense (or Depth):** The 1st defender slows the attacker with the ball, the 2nd defender recovers behind the 1st defender shutting down passing lanes and providing support (unless a double team is warranted), the 3rd defender will add balance to the group. The rest of the defenders will take up good positions and get compact, making it difficult to penetrate the defensive team shape.
3. **Concentration or Compactness:** The defenders will attempt to make the field smaller by intelligent positioning. When the field is made smaller the passing lanes close down, making possession and penetration very difficult.
4. **Balance**: After the 1st & 2nd defender the rest of the team takes part in defensive balance.

Training Principles

Each practice session should be conducted using specific training principles. These principles are in place to add structure, focus, organization and teaching methodology to the sessions. Using the principles in training will promote an overall better understanding of the training and how it relates to the game model.

1. **Principle of Complex Progression:** Going from simple to complex or small to large. Teaching the general topics of the game model, then moving into the more complex aspects of the game model. Do not move on to complex progressions if the simple aspects are not mastered.
2. **Principle of Propensities:** Training a specific important event or events over and over in a realistic way while maintaining the unpredictability of the actual game. Some coaches may call this using "triggers", just make sure the exercise stays realistic to the complexity of a real match.
3. **Principle of Specificity:** All exercises must be directly related to the game model. Training needs to be specific and focused.
4. **Principle of Horizontal Alternation Specificity:** Having some discontinuity in training to make sure fatigue levels do not get to high. Timing and monitoring of the rest to work ratio and calculating the overall workload for the day and week is critical for tactical periodization to be effective.
5. **Principle of Coaches Instinct**: The coach's ability to rely on his experience and education to make intelligent decisions when

training the team. Always listen to yourself and have the confidence to change things up.

Standard Morphocycle

The morphocycle is a standard weekly pattern of training designed to best prepare the players for a match at the end of the week. It is important for coaches to understand the morphocycle cycle and the reasons behind why it works. The weekly morpocycle is designed to be used each week for the entire season (making weekly changes if needed because soccer is a dynamic changing game). The goal is to stabilize a successful level of play each week (stabilization of performance). The Morphocycle works on the premise that full recovery for players is not possible until the fourth day after a top-level intense match. Recovery is not only physical but mental and emotional as well. It is also important to note that all games are different, some are much easier and some are much harder on the players. The coach will need to process the information from the previous week and create the subsequent morphocycle that makes sense. The coach's main goal is to stabilize successful high-level performances from the team on a week-to-week basis. Below is an outline of the 7-Day Morphocycle.

7-Day Morphocycle

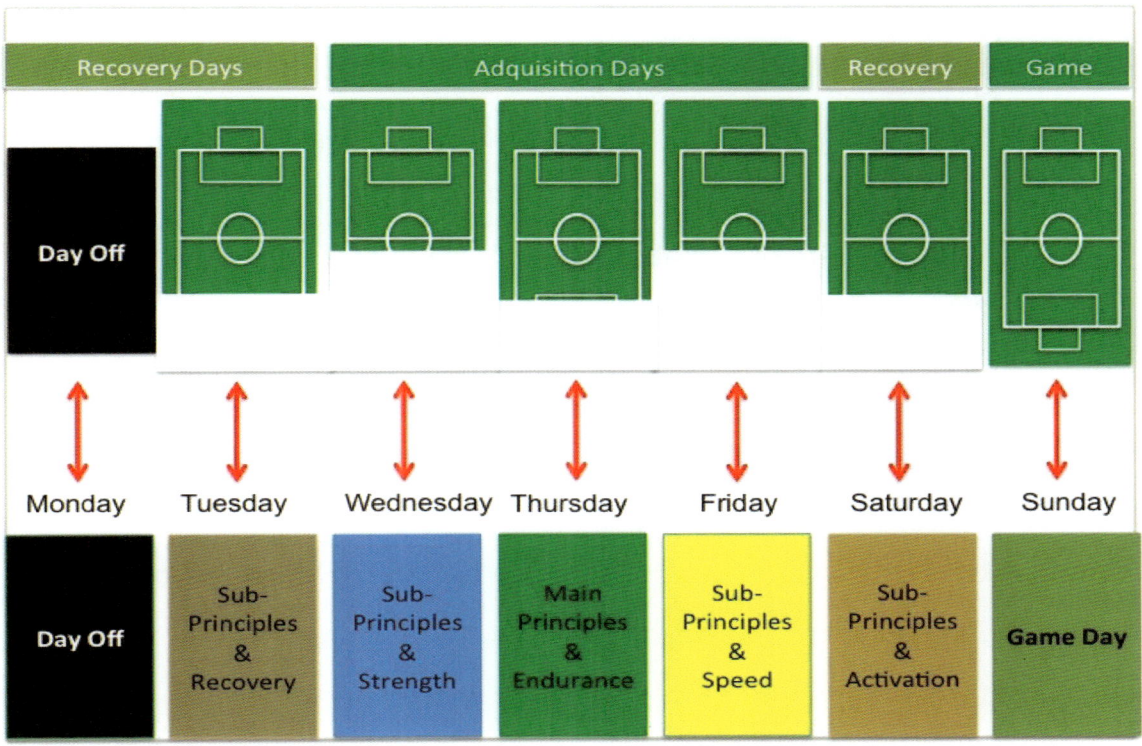

Details of 7-Day Morphocycle of Classic Tactical Periodization

Monday: Day of Rest In Tactical Periodization: The day of rest is the day following the game. The body and mind must have this day to recover and be ready for Tuesday.

Tuesday: Recovery Day "Specific" In recovery: Players will recover performing maximum effort in small sided games. The session may only be 45-60 minutes with 2 minutes work to 4 minutes rest ratio. Player's active playing time in the small-sided games will between 15-20 minutes. Emotionally "matches" require a lot of energy, so make this day of training less stressful and enjoyable. Tuesday is considered a recovery day in the training process. Players who played 30 minutes or less in the match should be separated and made to play a competitive game similar to the actual match from the weekend. This is needed to keep their fitness level high and overall sharpness.

Wednesday: Smaller numbers are used in the exercises but training is directly related to the game model. Practice focuses on working the sub-principles of the game model. The workload will be medium in duration but done at a high intensity. Strength is the physical aspect worked this day.

Thursday: This day will be the closest to a full 11v11 or 10v10 match setting. Larger numbers are used in training on ¾ of the field. Play is for around 10 minutes per/cycle, performing 4-6 cycles with 3-5 minute rest in-between each cycle. It is important not to fatigue the players too much on this day because "Match Day" is only 3 days away. The training on Thursday will work specifically on team concepts and will involve all the units together working collectively as a team (Keeper, Defense, Midfield and Forwards together). The complexity of the training is high (the total game model), the workload large and the physical aspect trained is endurance.

Friday: This is a day to guard against fatigue because it is just two days out from match-day. Fridays work concentrates on sub-principles as the complexity of training is decreased. The intensity levels can stay high but the duration and size of the field will be smaller. The physical aspect worked is speed.

Saturday: This is a recovery & general physical activation day. The day before a game is also used as a tactical review day of the materials covered during the week. The training will be short in duration with a reduced workload. The practice will be conducted in intervals with plenty of rest in between work intervals. The physical work should be at maximum speed, short duration and not involve many changes of direction. I like to have the players perform 4-6 short straight 8-yard sprints at maximum intensity at the end of training.

Sunday: Match Day

Adapting Tactical Periodization To Fit Your Coaching Situation

Tactical Periodization is used by Jose Mourinho, Andre Villas Boas, Brendan Rogers and many other top professional coaches at the highest level. The method works very well in the professional setting, having on average one match and five training sessions per/week with high level players. The weekly schedule does vary, but overall the professional game is 10 months long, made-up of weekly cycles (one game and five training sessions per/week). The question is can tactical periodization be adapted and used successfully in all kinds of different coaching situations? I am a college coach with a season that starts in August and ends in November. I don't have a very long time to establish a game model, teach set plays, get the team fit and develop a positive team culture. This doesn't even take into account my team will have to play a packed schedule with many back-to-back games. In order to win the "National Championship" in our division, it requires winning 4 games in 6 days. How do you even prepare a team to play 4 games in 6 days? These situations are not unique to college alone. High school and club soccer coaches face similar challenges. Whatever your current coaching situation is, I am confident tactical periodization can be adapted and used successfully with your team. One of the goals of this book is to provide coaches from different coaching situations flexible options that make sense in order to implement tactical periodization. The sample-morphocycle trainings below are meant to be an example of flexibility in the design of a weekly morphocycle. Tactical periodization is a very intelligent and sophisticated way to teach the game, structure your trainings and plan out your season, but it must be done in a way that makes sense for your current situation. I consider the tactical periodization model that I use to be a hybrid model. The adaptions I made are for three reasons. The first adaption is solely based upon the demands of the season and the schedule my team must play. The second adaption is to account for the level of the player I work with. Many players come into our program not having the experience or ability (mental or physical) to train at maximum intensity right away on a consistent basis. The last change is based on my personal soccer development philosophy. I place a value on certain training methods that are not directly linked to the game model or the player's field position. The three adaptions I made essentially customize tactical periodization to fit my unique coaching situation and soccer philosophy. I encourage you to experiment with the ideas presented and create the best version of tactical periodization for your own unique coaching situation.

One Week - Sample Training Plans For Standard Morphocycle

Tuesday Training

Focus: Low Complexity - Recovery

Work Load: Low

Physical Component: Recovery

Summary: Tuesday is the first day of training for the week with Sunday being game day and Monday being off. Tuesday's training should be intense but in short intervals and lots of recovery in between efforts. The total workload for the day will be small. The training exercises can be carried out using smaller grids, small-sided games and a focus on sub-principles of the game model. Players that played 30 minutes or less in the last game will train differently than the players who played above 30 minutes in the game. Players who played less than 30 minutes will be expected to play in a training match at a high intensity level (match does not have to be 90 minutes). This will allow those players to maintain their fitness and sharpness.

Modifications: If the game over the weekend was simple and not intense, training can be changed to be more complex and challenging. If the weekend match was very intense, emotional and physically taxing, the training can be minimal. On Tuesday I would discuss the major coaching points from the weekend's game and review the game film after training. The actual training would be broken up into exercises that are timed with a pre-set work and rest ratios (smaller work &

higher rest ratio this day), but I would also run some simple exercises without timing them. Take the training game called "Rondo" as an example. I may have the players play Rondo 8v2 in an 8 x 8 yard grid, but not timed and at a lesser intensity level. The speed of play always needs to be fast but the intensity can be less than full (partly because rondo does not require running from outside players). I want the players to focus and do their best but also to have fun and enjoy the rondo. Another example would be training cognitively challenging soccer exercises. Whenever I introduce a cognitive soccer exercise in which there are multiple rules and conditions placed on the players, it takes time for them to figure out solutions or the best way to play the game. Cognitive challenging games can be very difficult to play at full intensity, because players are trying to problem solve and figure out strategy. It would also be normal for me to add a passing pattern into Tuesdays training. Passing patterns would be timed or arranged as competitions between groups to ensure a high work rate. The main point is that part of training must be concerned with intensity, speed, workload & work rate, but other parts of training can to focus on aspects like problem solving, focus, speed of thought & concentration. This is one of the reasons why I call my model of tactical periodization a hybrid model.

Sample Training:
Cognitive Rondo: No Same Color Passing
Players: 12
Grid: 10x10 yards
Key points and Objectives:

The set-up is the same as fundamental rondo using a 10v2 shape. The 2 defenders in the middle are holding tennis balls in their hands. This lets the other players know they are the defenders. If a player gives possession away, the defender simply tosses the incoming player the tennis ball. The tennis ball simply replaces the tossing of the bib (tennis ball identifies the defenders). There are 6 different pairs of players in this game. Each pair is wearing a different color bib/vest than the other pairs. The rule of the game is players are not allowed to pass to the same color (their teammate). Your teammate might be next to you, on the other side of the circle or playing defense. It is crucial players identify the location of their teammate at all times. This will require players to think quickly and process additional information in order to be successful. Variation: require players to switch positions with the person they passed the ball to. This will make players continuously have to scan to locate their partner.

Exercise #2) Double Diamond Passing Pattern: This pattern can be done timed to ensure maximum intensity or as a competition against another group of players. For the competition, the first group to rotate the ball from the starting point and back five times is the winner. The diamond shape in the passing pattern exercise is viewed as two triangles. Triangles are the shapes we look for in our game model when holding possession of the ball. The passing patterns do work on sub-principles of the game model (positioning of teammates in support).

Description: Player A takes Player B's place, Player B takes Player C's place, Player C takes player D's place, Player D plays into Player E and fills E's spot. The rotation has to be timed right in order to develop the proper tempo in this pattern. Example: Player A and E must wait to rotate because they need to make the last pass to Player D & H. The shape of the exercise is two-diamonds.

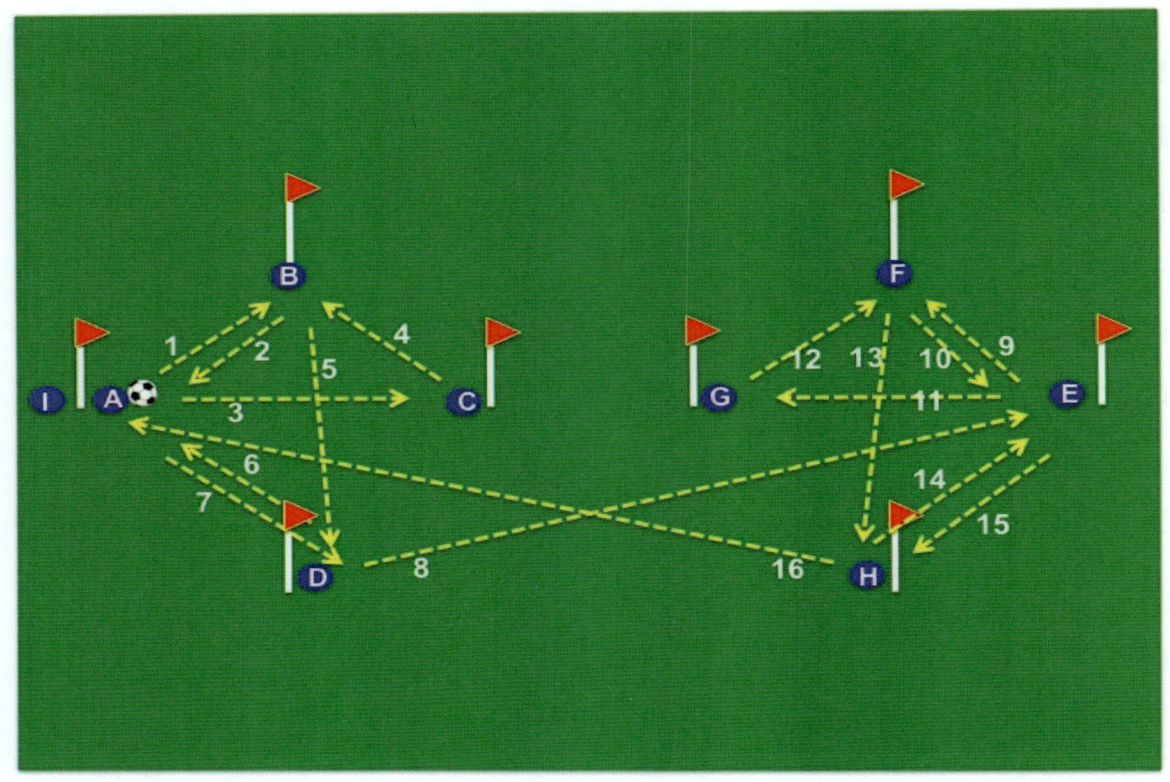

Exercise #3) Small Sided 4v4 Counter

Players: 8 players & 1 Coach (Coach Serves Balls From Side of Grid)

Key Points: The player that scores the goal must sprint behind the goal and around the cone before rejoining the game and helping his team defend. This small-sided game is relevant for a team that uses the counter attack as part of their game model. Many variations can be added – straight 4v4 with 4-6 small-sided cone goals or play 1-touch 3v3 with the extra 2 players that play as neutrals for both teams. Anytime variations are added they may change the workload and work rate, so monitor the changes and be sure the physical component of speed on this day is attained with a high intensity pace in small spaces. This small-sided game will be timed with a rest to work ration. Total small-sided game playing time would be between 14-22 minutes for a Tuesday.

Standard Morphocycle

Wednesday Training

Focus: Defensive Organization, Defensive Sub-Principles of The Game Model & Defensive Principles of Play

Work Load: Medium

Physical Component: Strength

Summary:

Players will still not be fully recovered from the match on Sunday, so Wednesday will be a medium workload day. Training will focus on the sub-principles of the game model, concentrating on specific units or sectors of the team (back line & midfield). The workload will be medium but the intensity level high. Training will be divided into work and rest intervals, so players will be rested enough to train at game realistic intensity levels.

Modifications: Wednesday is getting right into the middle of the week where the hard work really gets done. Training now uses larger numbers, larger grids, full goals and longer durations. Rondo is a staple in our curriculum and I make sure we train rondo 4-5 days a week in the beginning of training. We do this because we place a high value on the benefits of playing rondo, so we make the commitment to our rondo training. This is an adaption I make in my tactical periodization morphocycles to fit my own soccer beliefs. The sample session below is focused on defending so the next exercise after rondo leads right into defending. The entire defending practice is directly linked to how we defend in our 11v11 game model. We start with the back four as a unit and then add the midfield unit by the end of training. Splitting the team into units, groups or sectors can be a helpful way for players to learn (fractals). Teaching from small to large or unit to whole is great way for players to grasp the 11v11 game model. I would not hesitate to end the days training with a full 11v11 or 10v10 exercise to make the connection to the full game. The 11v11 exercise does not have to be long, as the workload for the day is supposed to be medium. The purpose of the 11v11 at the end is simply to make the connection from the unit or group training to the full game model. Playing 11v11 for a very small duration of time on Wednesday is another adaption I include in my program because I see value in it.

Sample Training
Sub-Principles: Compactness & Pressure, Cover & Balance

Exercise #1) Sliding Player Rondo: I

Players: 5v2 to 9v2

Grid: 10 yards x 10 yards in which players form circle. They can go outside the grid a foot or so but the idea is to keep the circle shape and not make the circle larger.

Key Points & Objectives:

Sliding rondo is simply rondo with a player who can slide into the middle and help keep the ball with the rest of the team. The middle player can either stay the entire time or take turns sliding in and out of the middle at any time. I like having the middle player sliding in and out as another player takes his spot in fluid motion without the game being stopped. It adds another layer of complexity and teamwork to the exercise.

Sliding Player Rondo

Exercise #2) Unit Defending Shape: Pressure, Cover & Balance

Players: 12

Grid: 40x30 yards (divided into 3 separate zones of 40x10 yards each)

Instructions & Key Points:

Three lines of four players each. The two teams in the end zones must try and pass the ball through the middle zone to the team in the far zone. The defending line of four players in the middle will be trying to stop any passes coming through. If the defending team in the middle wins the ball, play starts again with the ball in one of the end zone. Rotate the defending team out every 3 minutes. This exercise teaches 1st defender "pressure", 2nd defender "cover" and 3rd defender "balance". This is a single unit drill with four defenders working together to stop penetrating passes.

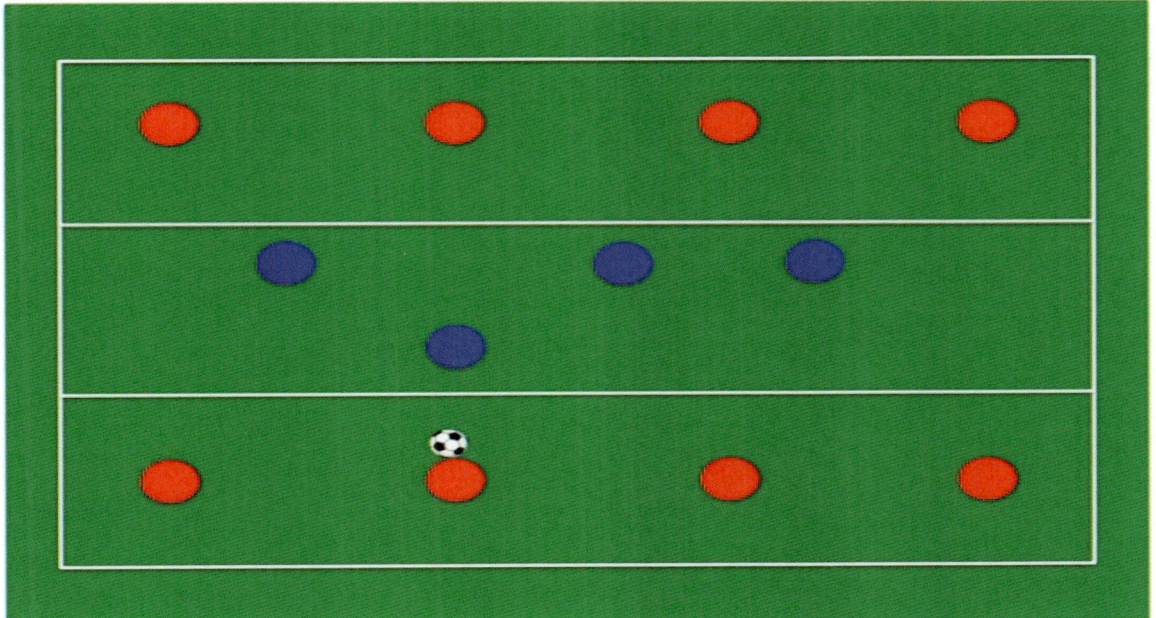

Exercise #3) 6v4 Unit Defending: Unit defending just like the game model.

Players: 13-18

Grid: Half Field

Instructions & Key Points:

6 attackers versus 4 defenders and a goalkeeper. The 6 attackers must be lined up in specific positions. 2 forwards, 2 wingers and 2 center midfielders who swing the ball from side to side and play into the forwards. The object is to move the ball quickly making the defensive line adjust to the movement of the players and ball. The end result of the attacker's possession should be a shot on goal (they can cross the ball as well). If the defenders win the ball they will attempt to play the ball out quickly to one of 2 target players. The coach will start a new ball at midfield at the end of each possession. The defensive line will be calling instructions like "ball", "slide right", "slide left", "push", "drop" and "hold". Offside rule is in effect. This exercise now trains the back four as a unit in a game realistic setting.

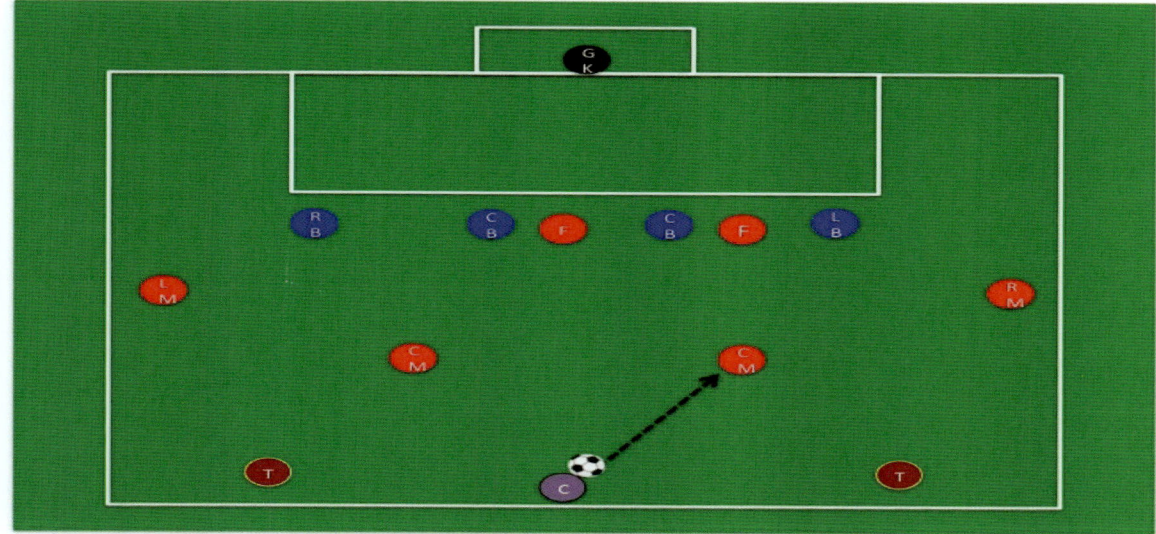

Exercise #4) 8v6 – Back 4 + 2 Center Midfielders (screening)
Players: 17-23
Grid: Half Field
Instructions & Key Points:
8 attackers versus 6 defenders and a goalkeeper. The 8 attackers must be lined up in specific positions. 2 forwards, 2 wingers, 2 center midfielders and 2 central defenders. The object is to move the ball quickly making the defensive line adjust to the movement of the players and ball. The end result of the attacker's possession should be a shot on goal (they can cross the ball as well). If the defenders win the ball they will attempt to play the ball out quickly to one of 2 target players. The coach will start a new ball at midfield at the end of each possession. The defensive line will be calling instructions like "ball", "slide right", "slide left", "push", "drop" and "hold". Offside rule is in effect. The 2 central midfield defenders should be 10-12 yards in front of the center backs. The 2 defending midfielders should stay more central and not get dragged out into wide positions. They are operating as a screen for the center backs, stopping balls from being played into the forward's feet. Establishing an effective low defensive 6-man block is essential for quality team defending in the 11v11 game model.

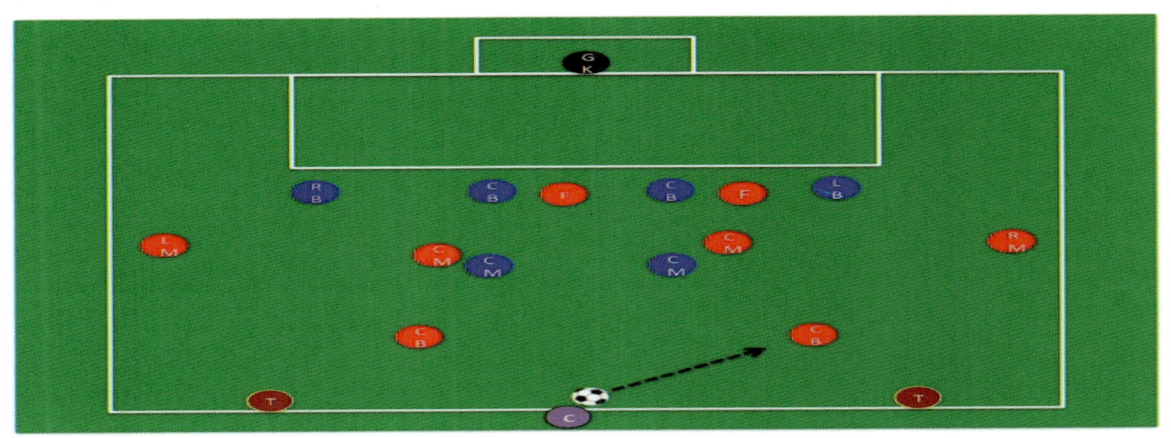

Exercise #5) 8v8 Game with Line of Confrontation

Players: 18

Grid: 50x60 yards

Instructions & Key Points:

8v8 with full goals and keepers. Each team will play with two lines of four. Both teams will play with a line of confrontation which they can't extend pressure over. The line of confrontation is 20 yards from the opponent's end line. The red line is the red teams line of confrontation and the blue line is the blue teams line of confrontation. Offside is in effect. Emphasize the coordination between lines, proper shape, compactness, problem and problem solving. Point out the importance of when the ball is lost regained. That point of transition is critical to each team. The attacking team wants to exploit the team who just lost the ball and the defending team needs to slow the ball down and get transition back to a compact shape. Pressure, cover and balance are always important points to make as well. This exercise allows the team to train the defensive moments of the game and the transitions that follow.

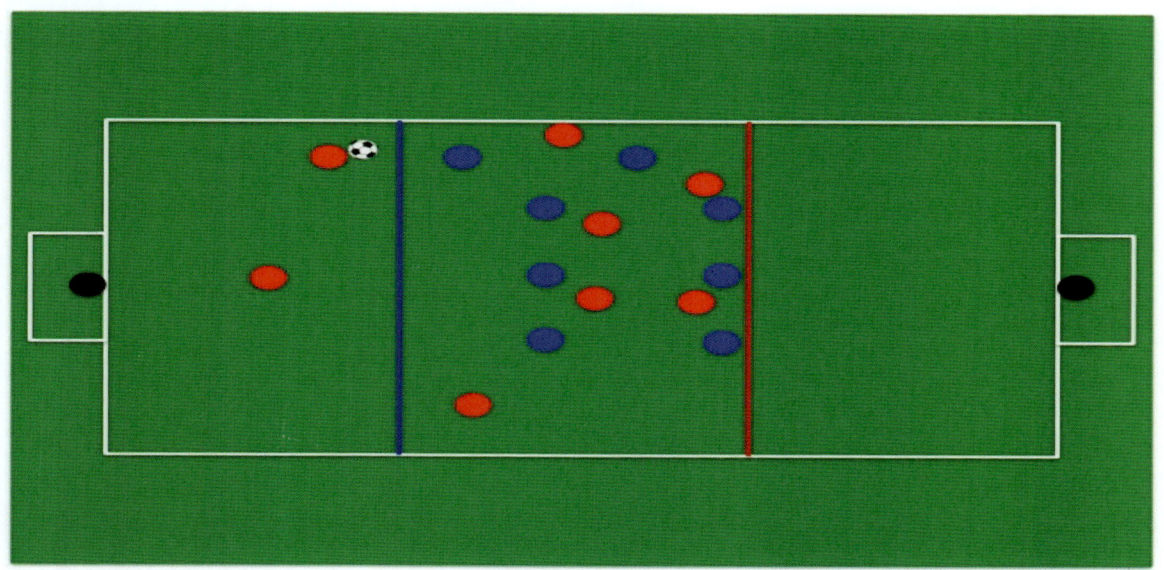

Standard Morphocycle

Thursday Training

Focus: 11v11 or 10v10 Game Model

Work Load: Large

Physical Component: Endurance

Summary: This day is the most intense day of training with the largest workload. Thursday will be a day to train with large numbers (9v9,10v10,11v11), training will be held in a larger area (half field to full field) and the work to rest ratio will be much higher on this day. Playing two 30 minutes halves of 10v10 on a 90-yard long field would be one option. The duration of training is longer and more continuous on Thursdays. Splitting the game into six or seven 10 minute playing periods with 2-3 minute breaks between is another option.

Modifications: Playing 11v11 is normally one of the most enjoyable training days for players. I carry 35 players on my team, so this day can be very challenging. I normally play my top 18 players about 60 minutes and rotate the others in. After playing 60 minutes the players will take part in 15-25 minutes of rondo, passing patterns or other lower intensity exercises that relate to our game model. For the 11v11 game we push one of the goals up 20-30 yards and use the free space to train the players who are waiting to join the game. It is important to monitor all 35 players workloads each week, which is no easy task.

When playing 11v11 have your starting team play against the formation the next opponent will likely use. As an option give the players in-game scenarios that require them to make adjustments: player down, player up, 10 minutes to play up a goal, 10 minutes to play down a goal etc. These types of variables can be added to the game without stoppages and disrupting the training. Short stoppages in the 11v11 will allow for attacking and defending restarts to be trained effectively in our game model. As the coach, you should always monitor the atmosphere and general feeling on the team. There will be times once in awhile when you can strip the structure from the training and just let the players have fun. I know this goes against the tactical periodization plan, but once in awhile setting up a three-team tournament is great for the players emotionally. Make the games 6 minutes each and keep score. After each team has played 60 minutes the tournament is over! Keep in mind Thursdays do not always have to be 11v11 either, feel free to work half field 8v8 or cross-field 9v9, but be sure the game model is being trained.

Sample Training:

Game like training with large numbers, close to full size field & full goals and keepers. Below are a couple ideas that can be worked into Thursday's training.

Exercise #1) One Team Zone Scoring

This 11 v 10 game uses a zone and a goal to score on. The blue team will score by passing the ball to a player running into the 7-yard zone. The red team will be scoring on the regular sized goal. The blue team will be scoring on the cross-field zone. The blue team will be able to exploit the red team if they use effective movement off the ball. The zone is much harder to defend than the goal because of the size of the zone. Teams should look to create attacking overloads to breakdown the defending team. Set the team up in the game model formation. This exercise is just one of many options that add some variety to 10v10 or 11v11 matches.

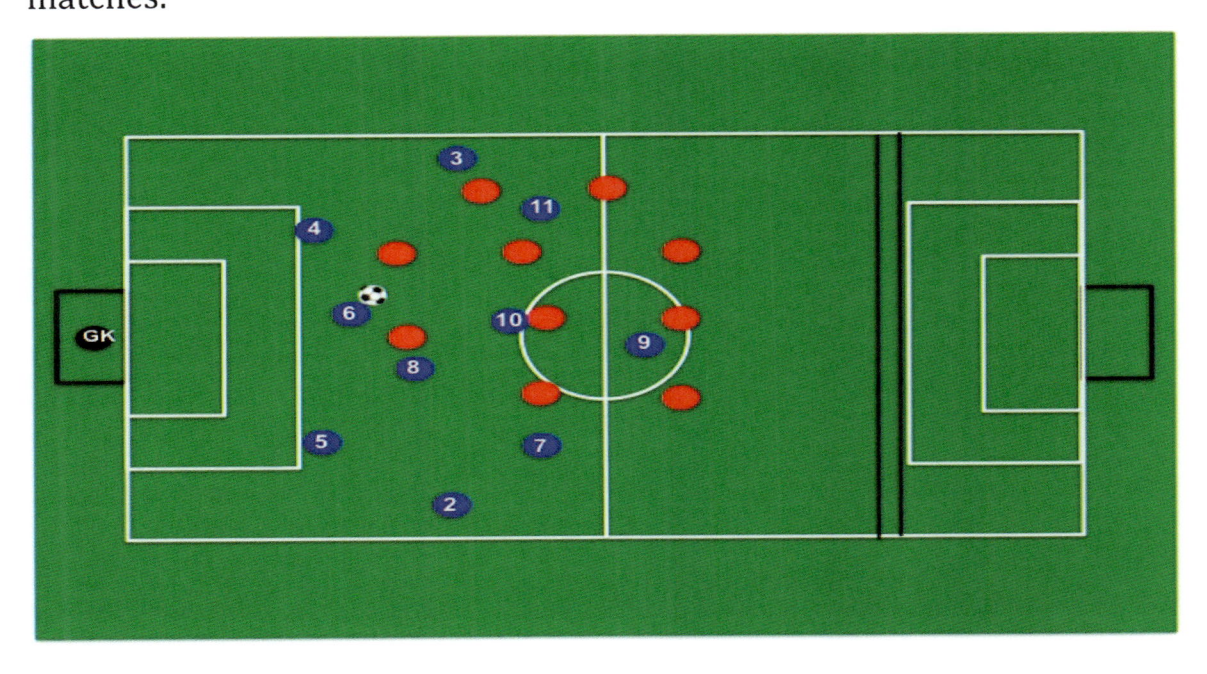

Exercise #2) Two Zone

This 10v10 game uses two cross-field zones for scoring. Teams score by passing the ball into the 7-yard zone to a teammate who is running into the zone and stops the ball. Because both zones are so wide, breaking down the defending team is possible with almost every possession (obviously will not happen every possession). Attacking overloads should be created to break down the defending team. Make sure the formation and roles are specific to the game model. This is another variation for 10v10 training. I normally play 5 minutes 3-touch, 5 minutes 2 touch and 5-minutes 1 touch. After the 15 minutes I will progress into a match with full goals and keepers.

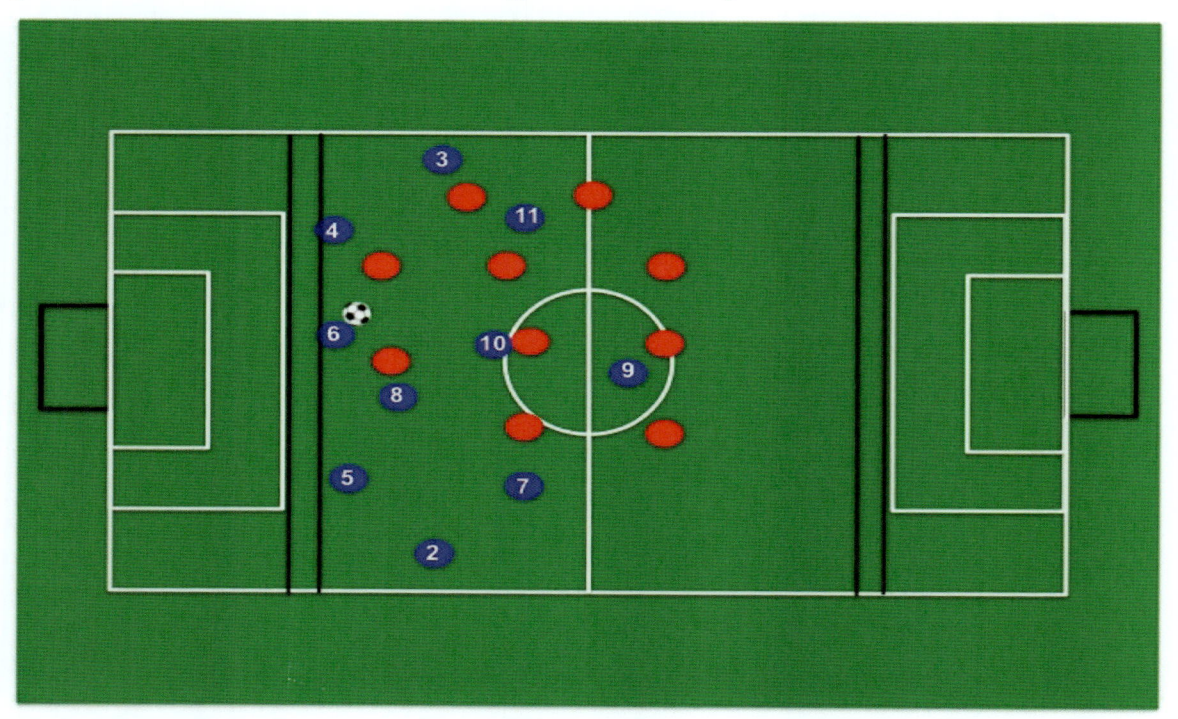

Standard Morphocycle

Friday Training

Focus: Offensive Organization: Sub-Principles of The Game Model

Work Load: Medium-Lower

Physical Component: Speed

Summary: Because the match is only a couple days away and Thursday was the hardest training day of the week, it is important to cut down on the workload for Friday and guard against fatigue. The sub-principles of the game model will be the focus of training.

Modifications: The game is now two days out and the workload for the day is determined by how the players feel and the opponent you are playing on Sunday. In general the workload should be medium to lower this day. Sub-principles of the game model are the focus for this day. This sample training below focuses on attacking organization sub-principles of the game.

Sample Training:

Exercise #1) Arsenal FC - 10v2

Simple keep-away game that demands speed of thought & quick passing. Moving the ball 1-touch & playing quickly fits directly into the game model.

Players: 9v2 or 10v2 or with less numbers go 6v1 to 8v1.

Grid: 10 yards x 10 yards. No player allowed outside the grid. It is important to keep the space tight and only 10x10.

Key Points & Objectives:

The game is 1 touch only. Players should not be in a circle like rondo. They need to be moving inside the grid all the time on the balls of their feet ready to play one touch. The two defenders have the bibs/vests in their hands and try to win the ball. If a defender wins the ball or it goes outside the grid he throws the bib to the players who gave the ball away. The game should not be stopping. Have a coach outside feeding balls in right away as soon as the ball is hit out of the grid. Arsenal FC uses this drill and it is one of my personal favorites. It teaches quick play, one touch passing and movement off the ball. This 10v2 one touch game is played in the same 10x10 grid as your rondo so the transition is seamless.

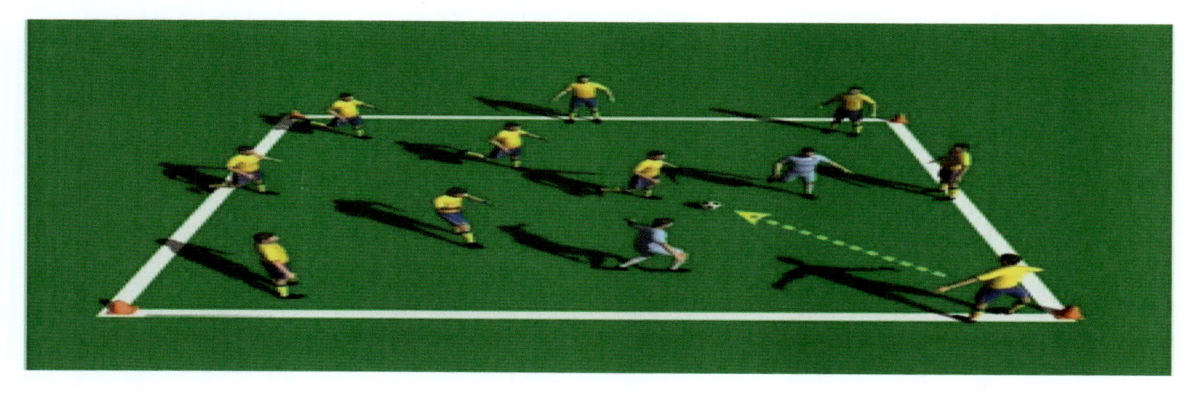

Exercises #2) Two-Team Shadow Play: This exercise can be used to teach attacking patterns and movements. It directly relates to the movements we want to occur in the actual game. The exercise is a low intensity but can become complex if the coach adds various conditions. The blue team attacks one goal moving the ball down the field as the red team does the same attacking the other goal. The teams must be aware and avoid each other while executing their attacking movements passing the ball. After each team finishes on goal, they will jog back to the other side of the field and build a new attack. Emphasize coordinated movement, passing the ball to all lines, establishing a good passing rhythm, demanding constant communication between players and finishing each attacking movement with a quality shot on goal. Two-team shadow play is an effective way to teach attacking movement for a specific game model.

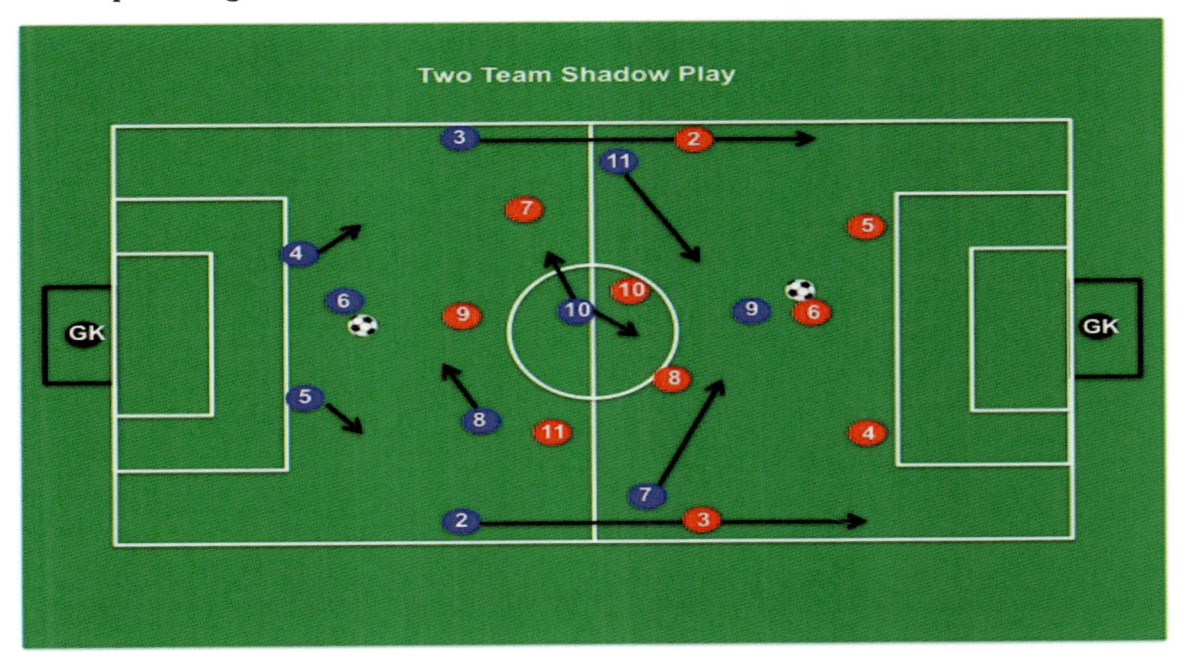

Exercise #3) 6v6+keeper Phase Play – Working on Attack in The 4-2-3-1 Game Model

The red team is trying to score on the keeper while the blue team is looking to score on either small goal. The red team will be encouraged to interchange movements when in possession. In order to keep the focus on the red attacking team, the blue team must score within 5 or less passes after a turnover. The red team is set-up position specific to the 4-2-3-1 (2 wingers, forward, attacking and passing center midfielders).

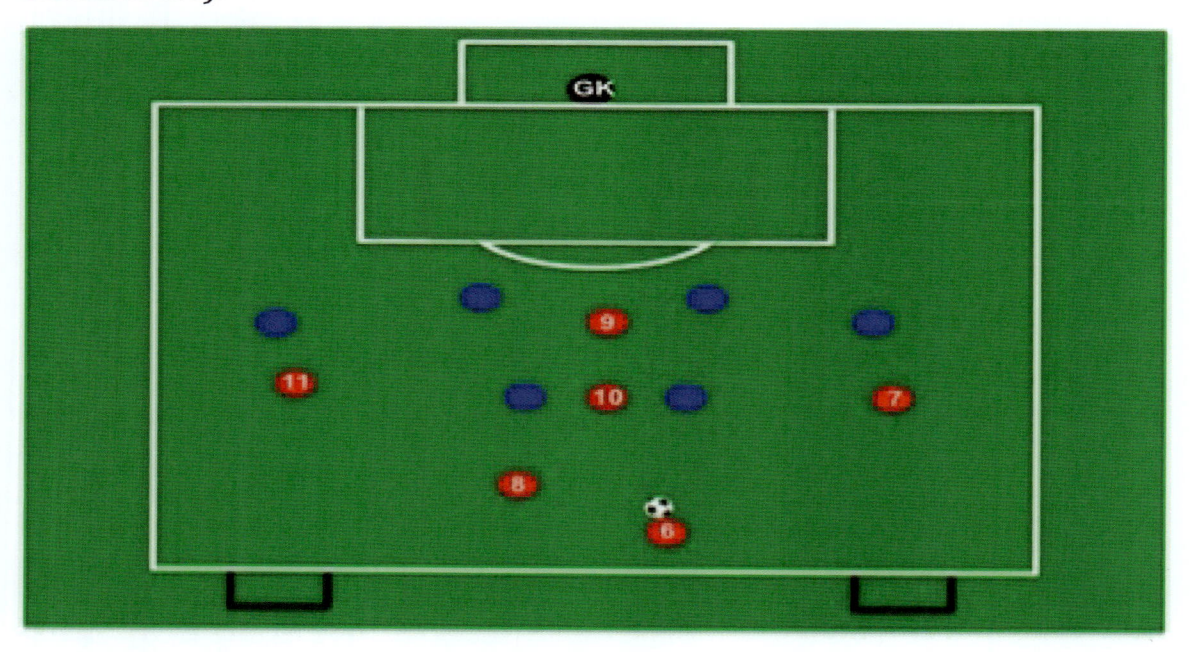

Exercise #4) 8v6, 8v7 & 8v8 Zone 14 – Specific To The 4-2-3-1 Game Model

This exercise is the same as exercise#3, but the numbers progress from 6v6 to 8v6 (can work up to 8v8). The outside wingbacks are now included, adding width to the attack. Red scores on the keeper and blue has 5 passes or less to score on either of the small sided goals at midfield. Try the exercise with and without the "Zone 14". This exercise works on attacking organization in 4-2-3-1 game model.

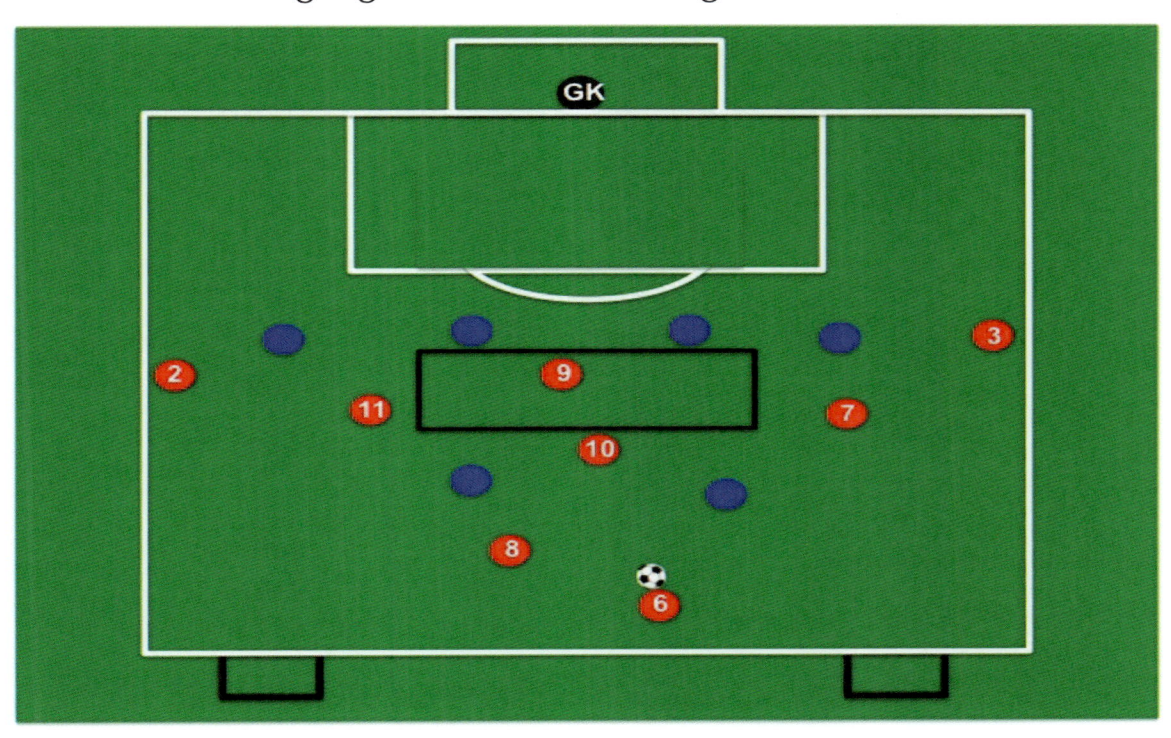

Exercise #5) Compact Field: 3-2-1-Touch

This 11v11 or 10v10 game is played 2/3 of the field using the width of the penalty box. The compact field makes movement and finding space difficult for the attacking team. The smaller space will force players to be even sharper and more coordinated in their movement off the ball. Play 5 minutes 3-touch, 5 minutes 2-touch and 5 minutes 1-touch. The specific formation of the game model will be used in the training. The space and touch restrictions make this exercise less demanding than an actual match. This exercise would be done the last 15 minutes of training.

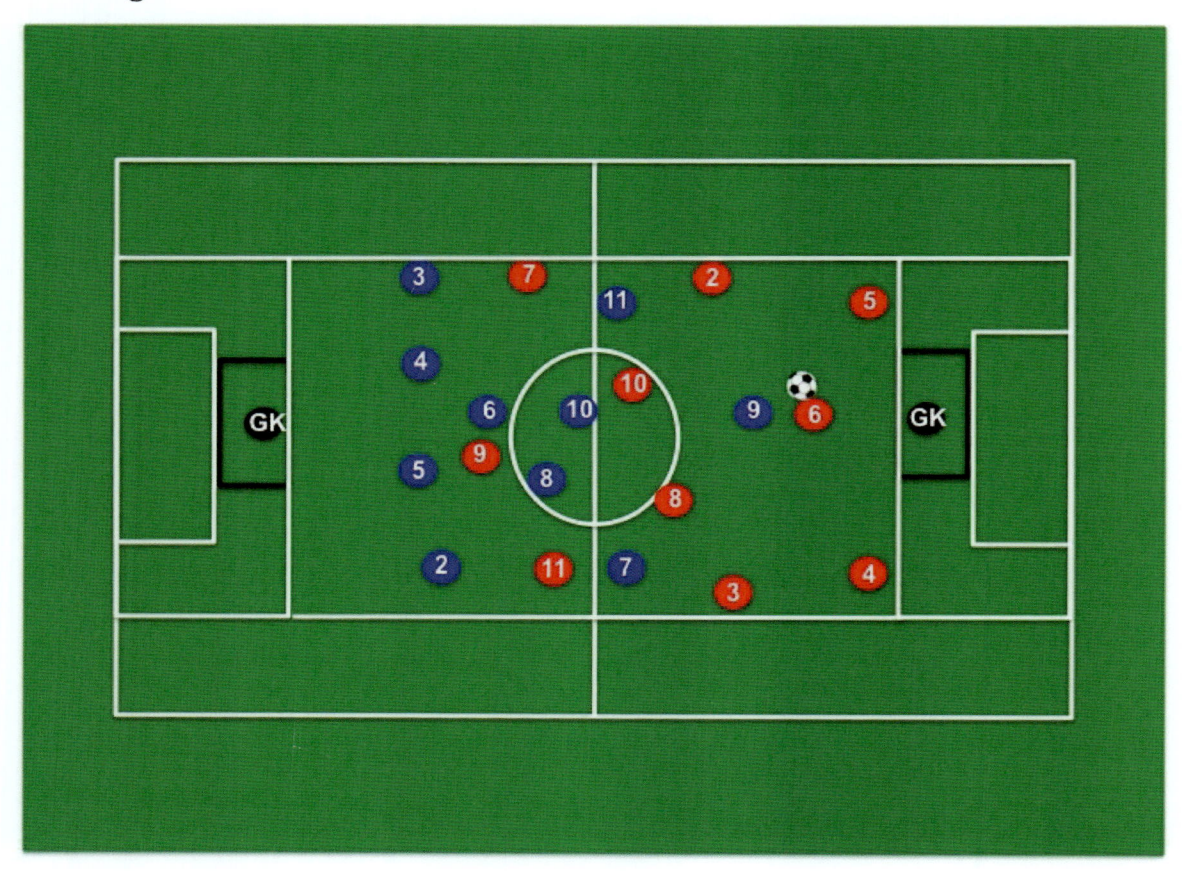

Standard Morphocycle

Saturday Training

Focus: Focus on Tactical Review of Game Model & Activation of Body

Work Load: Low

Physical Component: Activation

Summary: This is a very light training day and serves as a review for match tactics and the week's work. The atmosphere at practice should be fun and energetic the day before a game. It is important to incorporate some high intensity short duration movements to activate the body (straight-line accelerations with limited direction changes).

Modifications: Our day before workouts always involve fun competitions between the players and sometimes even the coaches! Saturday's training starts out with a complete warm-up that works into fun competitions. Once the players have enjoyed themselves in some fun soccer 4-square or soccer tennis competitions, we continue with very challenging short intensity small-sided 1or 2-touch games. These games are set-up in our game model formation. The next part of training is finishing/shooting and than a quick review of any last tactics for the match along with some sprints. The shooting/finishing exercises are constructed to provide ample rest in between repetitions (in order to reduce fatigue and chance of injury). The training is concluded with 4-6 short straight-line full intensity sprints of 8-yards each. Any last tactical points are covered at the conclusion of training. Much of what we do the day before the game does fit the game model and sub-principles. However, my main concern is that players are feeling rested, excited and well prepared leading into the up coming match.

Sample Training:

Players: 10-14

Grid: 18x18 yards (divided into 9x9 yard squares)

Soccer 4-Square: Fun Game – Can Improve 1st Touch

This is a fun game where the serving team stays on until they lose. If the serving team loses they will rotate out and the team from square #3 will rotate and become the new servers. All teams will rotate one space forward if possible after a point is won. The team that was waiting enters square #1 after a point is scored. The rules of the game are as follows: serving has to be on an arc off a bounce from the designated area to any square, players are allowed 1-touch each, no spiking. Variations: both partners must touch the ball before passing it to another square, have three players per/square, play 1-touch per/person.

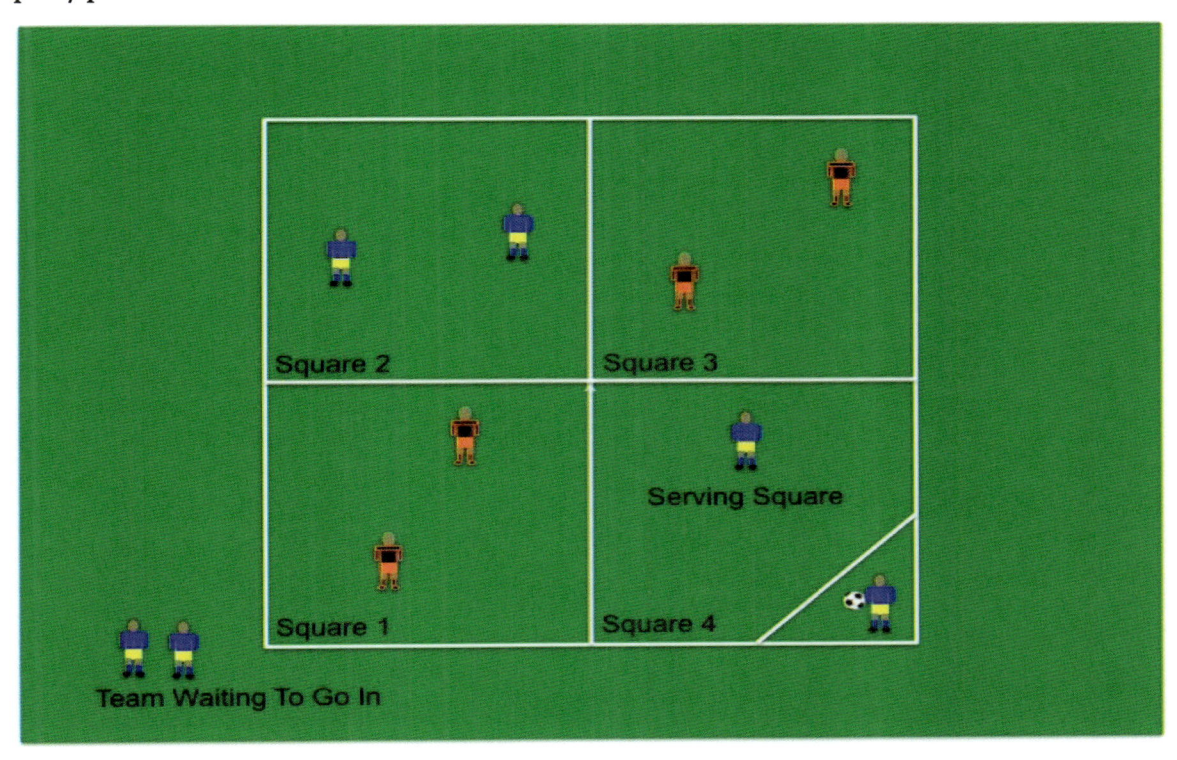

Speed 1-2 Touch Small Sided Game:

This exercise is done using the same formation as the game model (we use a 4-2-3-1 formation)

Players: 17-18 players

Grid: 35 yards long x 25 yards wide. You can feel free to change the grid size depending on your objectives. If you want the players to be under a lot of pressure then keep the grid small, if you want them to run a bit more then make the grid larger. Experiment and see what you like.

Key Points & Observations:

This is a touch two game with players set up in position specific spaces on the field. Each team has two center backs, two outside wing backs, defensive center mid, passing center mid, attacking center mid and a forward. There is also one neutral player on the field playing for the team in possession. The neutral player helps the ball move swiftly. The objective is to move the ball from your backs through the midfield and to your forward. Once the forward receives the ball, the team will attempt to move the ball back to the defenders without losing possession. Once possession is lost, players must work hard to get the ball back. Both teams are set up the exact same way trying to accomplish the same tasks. Outside players are located in safe zones so inside players can't come out of the field and take the ball from outside players. The teams on the inside can only play to their own players on the outside. The ball moves very fast in this game, it is directly game related to many of the rondo skills attained in training.

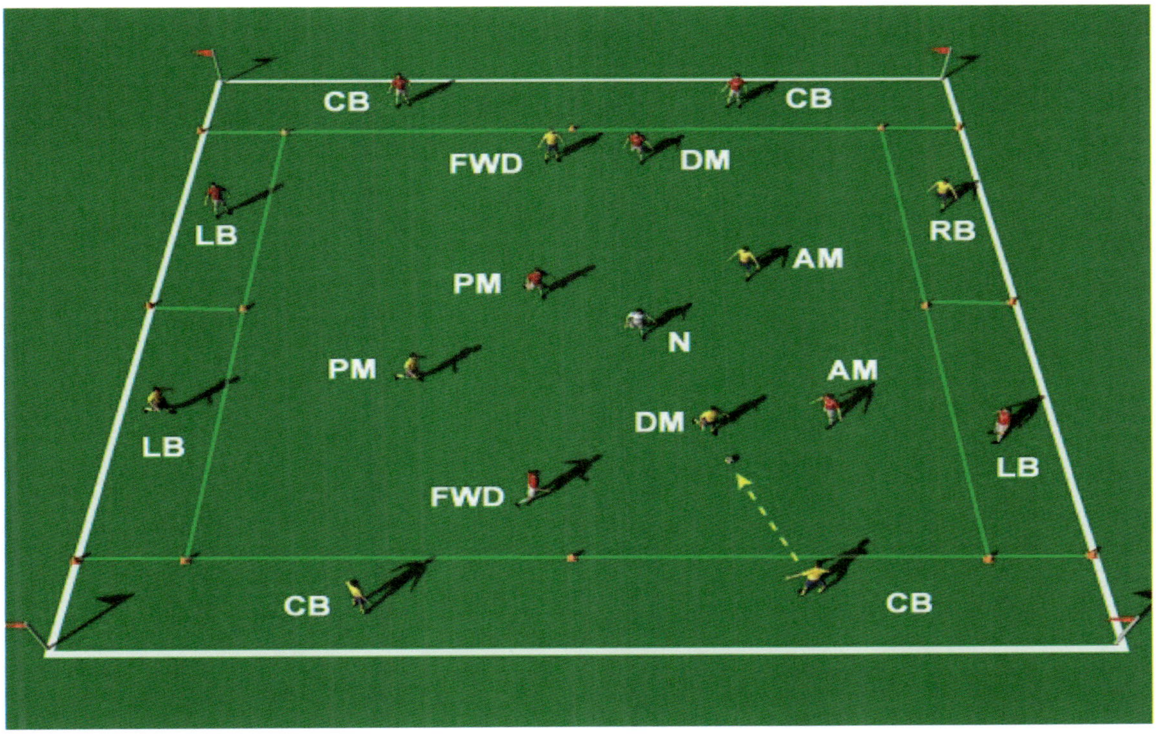
CB
CB
FWD
DM
LB
RB
PM
AM
N
PM
AM
LB
DM
LB
FWD
CB
CB

Passing Pattern Shooting:

I like to incorporate shooting a few days a week. This shooting drill allows for amble rest between reps and also works on passing. The more players added to the drill the more rest players will get. Saturdays practice is all about finishing the last tactical details for the match and having fun, being ready for the match on Sunday.

Grid: 45x345 yards

Instructions & Key Points:

In this passing pattern players rotate forward one position with each repetition. Firm passing to the correct foot is required. Passes #1-5 can be 1-touch with the final shot #6 being 1 or 2-touch. Coordination, rhythm and timing between the groups are essential for this exercise to work well. Vary the set-up of the cones of the last shot in order to change the distance and angles for the shooter. This will force the shooter to adapt his shot & technique.

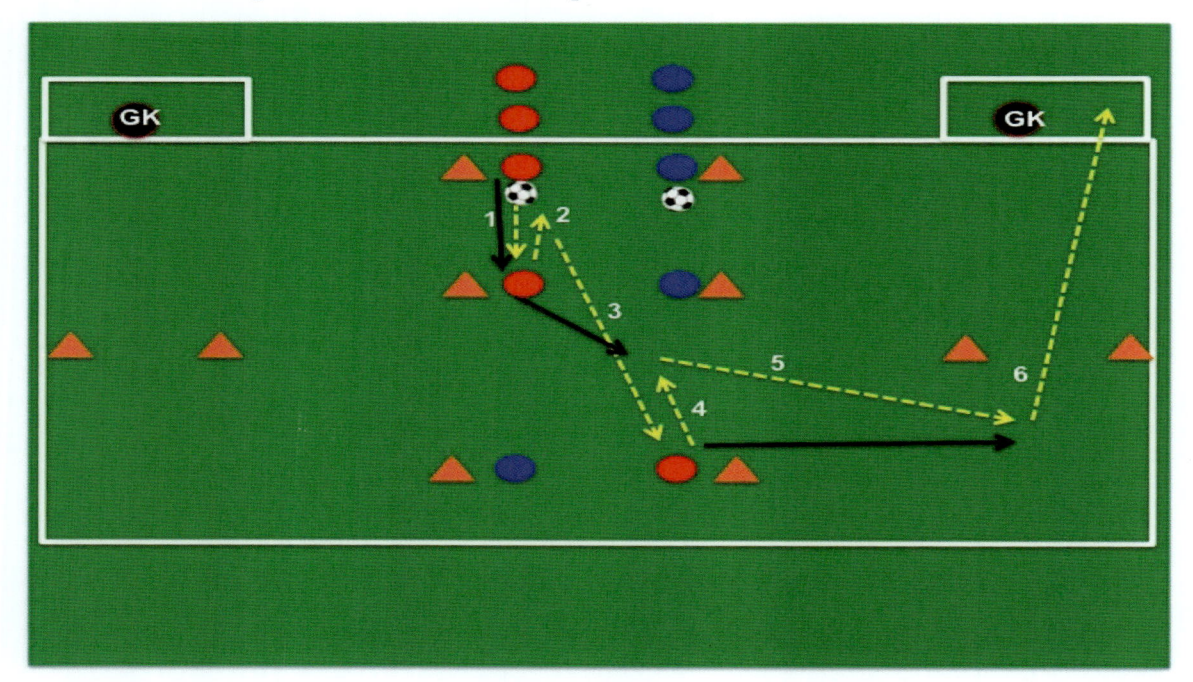

Saturdays practice is finished with 4-6 high intensity sprints of 8-yards each with 30 seconds rest in between.

I hope you enjoyed my take on tactical periodization. I always look forward to hearing your thoughts and or questions. Feel free to email me at coachdibernardo@gmail.com Also, be sure to check out my blog at www.coachdibernardo.com and my cognitive soccer website at www.soccersmarttraining.com   My author central page has a listing of all my books, audio books and videos that are available on amazon.com.

References

1. Tactical Periodization "A Practical Application for the Game Model of Bayern Munich of Jupp Heynckes(2013-14)..By Pedro Mendonca..Copywright 2013-2014
2. Soccer "Developing A Know-How"..By Carlos Carvalhal..Copywright 2014..Prime Books

Printed in Poland
by Amazon Fulfillment
Poland Sp. z o.o., Wrocław